Lancing College Chapel

LANCING COLLEGE was founded by the Revd Nathaniel Woodard, curate at Shoreham-by-Sea, in 1848. In his 'Plea for the Middle Classes' Woodard had argued the need for more, and less exclusive, independent schools. In these 'the teaching and practice of the Catholic faith, as it is expressed in the Book of Common Prayer', was to be central. Dedicated to Saints Mary and Nicolas, after the beautiful ancient churches of Shoreham, the school moved to its present position in 1857. The Founder believed in the educational value of 'correct buildings' and employed R.C. Carpenter as architect of the college. It was his son R.H. (Herbert) Carpenter and his partner William Slater who completed the design for the chapel as the place of worship for Lancing College and the Central Minster of all the schools founded by Woodard or associated with his foundation.

The style of the chapel was described by Sir George Oatley as 'a perfect blend between the lightness and elegance of the early French Gothic and the strength and muscularity added to it on the soil of England'. The foundation stone was laid in 1868 and the building was done by resident masons. Foundations up to 21m (70ft) deep hold the chapel on its spectacularly eminent site. It is built of Sussex sandstone from Scaynes Hill. From its completion in 1875 the crypt was used by the school, until the upper chapel was consecrated on 18 July 1911. Even then the tower, originally planned to be 107m (350ft) high, and the west end were not built. In 1947 the Friends of Lancing Chapel commissioned a new design for the west end from Stephen Dykes Bower. His west wall and rose window were dedicated in 1978, but this remarkable building, intended by its Founder as a symbol of faith and a challenge to materialism, remains incomplete.

⌐ The unfinished west end, showing the doors and arches which will be sheltered by the proposed porch attached to the bricked-up elevations.

➢ Alan Rome's 'artist's impression' of his design for a west porch to complete the chapel, which the Friends of Lancing Chapel now plan to build.

The West Front

Approaching the west front of the chapel the visitor will notice walls shored up with common brickwork, temporary doors and arches boarded over. It is obviously unfinished. Plans for an ante-chapel linking the chapel to the school buildings are no longer practical. But an elegant porch, designed by the late chapel architect Alan Rome OBE FRIBA, is a realistic alternative. A foundation stone, laid by the Founder's great-grandson in 2011, affirms the Friends' determination to complete the chapel by building the porch. We ask every visitor to contribute something to this inspirational project. At the north-west corner can be seen the foundations of the tower which Carpenter and Woodard originally intended but which will not now be built. The west wall is of Somerset limestone which weathers better than the local sandstone.

◁ The narthex crossing the west end, designed and ornamented by Stephen Dykes Bower.

▷ The south-west window commemorating Father Trevor Huddleston OL, designed and made by Mel Howse.

The Entrance

Entering the chapel at the west end, you are in that part of the chapel designed by Stephen Dykes Bower and dedicated by Archbishop Coggan, in the presence of HRH The Prince of Wales, on 13 May 1978. The names of the foremen of Messrs J. Longley, who built the award-winning west wall, are inscribed on the stone. An elm-wood statue of Our Lady, carved by Leonard Ratcliffe, watches over the entrance, where two temporary doors fill arches which will one day open into the porch. At the south end, beyond the Verger's office, is a stained-glass window designed and made by Mel Howse of Chichester in honour of Archbishop Trevor Huddleston, a former pupil of Lancing who campaigned against apartheid in South Africa. The window was installed in 2007 and dedicated by Archbishop Desmond Tutu, as recorded on a stone let into the floor.

In the north-west corner is the Golden Book, recording all those who by their skills or subscriptions contribute to the building of the chapel. Steps lead down to the crypt and up to the pulpitum. The organ loft gate, made by Norman Furneaux, was decorated by Campbell Smith and Co., as was the painted ceiling, a modern expression of medieval design with deliberately subdued tones to emphasise the effect of light and space as you turn through the central arch into the nave.

The Nave and High Altar

The first impression of the nave is its height: 27m (90ft) to the apex of the vault. It is said to be the fourth tallest ecclesiastical building in Britain. The clusters of the columns rise outside the triforium between simply moulded bases and capitals, emphasising the vertical lines. Light from the exceptionally tall clerestory windows is reflected from the stone-ribbed vault, which is filled with chalk quarried near the school. The triforium has a double line of trefoil arches with carved cusps and latticework, and is pierced with windows over the altar. The floor is of Portland stone salvaged from a barquentine wrecked off Shoreham in the 1870s.

The stalls at the sides of the nave were designed by Walter Tower, and their canopies, by Gilbert Scott, were presented to Lancing by Eton College. The chairs were given by the boys at the school in 1911 and brass plates recall those who fell in the First World War. The chandeliers, by Dykes Bower, were added in the 1980s. The brass lectern, by Bainbridge Reynolds, is in memory of Edmund Field (Chaplain 1853–92).

The high altar which was inscribed with golden Christian symbols to mark the second millennium is approached by several varied flights of steps. Beside the sanctuary are canopied stalls for the Provost and the Bishop. The bronze candlesticks are early eighteenth-century copies of a pair by Annibale Fontana in the Certosa at Pavia. The high altar cross is Toledo silverware of about 1490, given by Martin Gibbs with candlesticks by Bainbridge Reynolds.

➤➤ The nave looking east with the patronal banner by Sir Ninian Comper leading the procession at the end of a school service.

⋎ The Eucharist is celebrated at the high altar.

The Organs

Music is an essential part of worship and Lancing has a strong choral and instrumental tradition. Two organs can be seen from the high altar steps. At the west end is the organ originally built for the chapel in 1914 by J.W. Walker. It was rebuilt and completed by Walkers and voiced by Paul Fulger in 1986. It has four manuals, 70 drawstops and 3,509 pipes with great organ reeds en chamade in the manner of Cavaillé-Coll; it weighs over 20 tonnes and rises 11m (36ft) above the gallery floor. The smaller instrument next to the choir stalls is by the Danish firm Th. Frobenius. Built in 1986 with two manuals, 25 drawstops and 1,370 pipes, it was voiced by Mogens Pedersen.

The organs are independent and distinctive instruments, each with tracker action, but they are linked electronically by a multicore cable so that the west organ can be played in part from the choir. The Frobenius is best suited to the classical repertoire and is used to accompany the liturgy; the Walker retains its traditional 'English' sound and supports the congregation. Together they can produce antiphonal effects or fill the chapel with music.

The cases of both organs were designed by David Graebe with decorative oak carving by Derek Riley. On the choir organ the arms of Lancing and the Chichester diocese are set in tracery, surrounded by roses and lilies, the emblems of the Blessed Virgin Mary, celebrating the position of the instrument beside the Lady Chapel. The foliage of the pipe shades echoes the much larger oak leaves and acorns carved in the west case, which also incorporates owls, nuthatches, woodpeckers, squirrels, and Sussex martlets swooping around the central towers. The front pipes of the Frobenius are of polished tin, reflecting light from the chandeliers and windows; those of the Walker are zinc sprayed with bronze particles, giving a rich warmth to the west end as the pedal towers lead the eye up to the rose window, which is described later.

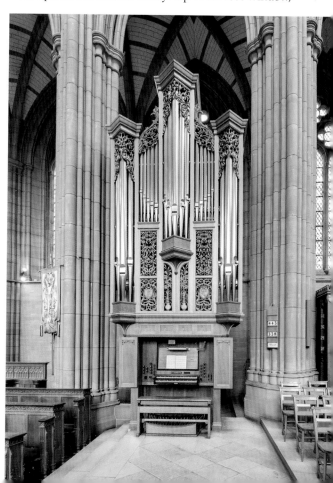

The organs were installed in consultation with Alan Rome, chapel architect in the 1980s, who designed the organ screens in the aisles. An inaugural recital was given by Carlo Curley in 1986.

In the crypt there is a chamber organ of 1818 by Thomas Elliott of London. The instrument has a classical mahogany case, with gilded front pipes. It was originally housed in Hawarden Castle and was given to Lancing by Sir William Gladstone, former Head Master, and fully restored by Saxon Aldred in 1987.

◄ The nave looking west; the rose window and chandeliers by Dykes Bower; the organ by J.W. Walker, 1914, rebuilt 1986.

➤ The choir organ by Frobenius, 1986.

The Tapestries

The Lancing Tapestries were designed by Amy Lady Chilston in 1933, as a substitute for the massive reredos originally planned. They were woven on the great loom at Merton Abbey, which had been set up by William Morris, and were completed by 1937. Among the figures in the tapestries are the patron saints of many of the Woodard Schools, some with their attributes, in settings of Gothic architecture with angels. The fountain in the centre is the symbol of the four rivers of Paradise, and the foreground is filled with colourful birds and wild flowers.

LEFT PANEL
Top border: Saint Andrew; an Angel; Saint Peter; an Angel; Saint James the Great. Lower border: Saint Thomas; an Angel; Saint Paul; an Angel; Saint James the Less. Central figures: Saint John the Evangelist; the Virgin Mary; Saint Anne.

CENTRAL PANEL
Top border: Saint Matthew; emblem of Saint Matthew; emblem of Saint John; Saint John. Lower border: Saint Luke; emblem of Saint Luke; emblem of Saint Mark; Saint Mark. Central figures: Saint Michael; Our Lord in Glory; Saint Nicolas.

RIGHT PANEL
Top border: Saint Bartholomew; an Angel; Saint Philip; an Angel; Saint Simon. Lower border: Saint Matthias; an Angel; Saint Thaddeus; an Angel; Saint Barnabas. Central figures: Saint Cuthbert; Saint John the Baptist; Saint Ethelburga.

The Saint Nicolas Chapel

Turning into the south aisle, you enter the Saint Nicolas Chapel. There is a seventeenth-century Flemish carved wood figure of the saint in the sedilia, and the corbels of the canopy above show his symbol, the apple, carved by J.C. Blair. The silver pendant lamp is Spanish. The window over the altar, by Sir Ninian Comper, represents Saints Martin and Nicolas, and is in memory of Provost Bishop Southwell and Henry Martin Gibbs of Tyntesfield, who was one of the greatest benefactors of the college. All the south and north aisle windows have been glazed with leaded lights and tinted glass quarries in memory of former pupils, teachers, friends and benefactors of Lancing. Pause to read the brass memorial to Edmund Blackmore, the first bursar. The Founder's Chantry, in rich Perpendicular ogee style, was designed by Temple Moore. It contains a reredos by Comper, memorials to Woodard's wife Eliza and their children, and a recumbent bronze figure of the Founder himself by P. Bryant Baker (1915), resting on a slab of Sussex marble. This chapel is reserved for private prayer. The south doors were given by Canon John Hayter OL in Lancing's 150th year. The White Ensign at the west end of the aisle recalls the use of the college as HMS *King Alfred* by the Royal Navy for training during the Second World War.

The Saint Nicolas Chapel in the south aisle, with a window by Sir Ninian Comper; the Founder's Chantry by Temple Moore is on the left.

The interior of Billy Woodard's chantry chapel in the north aisle.

The Lady Chapel

To appreciate the purity of its lines and the elegance of its proportions, it is best to enter the north aisle from the west end. On the right there are cases containing a Bruce Rogers bible, printed in 1935, and a First World War Roll of Honour. Notice the hatchment of the Thorold arms and the armorial windows in memory of Lord Trevelyan, whose Garter banner is displayed elsewhere in the chapel, and Sir Robert Megarry. On the north wall is a Russian icon portraying Saint Veronica's handkerchief given in memory of William Russell, an early choir master of Lancing. The framed needlework is the original school banner.

In the bay beyond the organ is an oak chantry chapel, by Temple Moore, remembering W.B. ('Billy') Woodard, third son of the Founder, who dedicated his life to carrying out his father's wishes and, as master builder of the chapel, realised Carpenter's designs in stone. Fittingly, the stonework of the Lady Chapel's east window was the gift of Hugh Knight, Clerk of the Works, in the 1870s. The stained glass by Stephen Dykes Bower, which honours Our Lady in its inscription, commemorates all those who have worked on the chapel. The six lozenges, on a grisaille background, represent, on the left, the carpenter's shop at Nazareth; the architect and Founder (centre); laying the foundation stone (bottom); and on the right, glassmaking (top); constructing the rose window (centre); and the Eucharist of Dedication. Below are emblems of Saints Mary and Nicolas, and above, the completed chapel seen from the north-east.

In the sedilia, which are ornamented with carved lilies, is a picture of the Agony in the Garden by Linnell presented in memory of Esther Neville Smith by Peter Pears (once a chorister here) and Benjamin Britten, who wrote his cantata *Saint Nicolas* for the centenary of the school. The painting over the altar was given by the Revd Tom Selwyn Smith. Details of other paintings will be found on their frames.

The embroidery of the stall cushions and kneelers was done by various friends of the chapel and college residents. The designs, by Sir William Gladstone, incorporate crosses and other appropriate Christian symbols. Processional banners of the chapel's patron saints (designed by Sir Ninian Comper) and of the holy sacraments are on display.

◁ The north aisle looking towards the Lady Chapel, furnished by Dykes Bower.

The Rose Window and the Woodard Schools

Return to the altar steps to observe the more recent western bay of the chapel, built in Doulting limestone and furnished with oak stalls made by H. and K. Mabbitt. There are armorial carvings in the oak and stone. The outstanding feature of Dykes Bower's design is the rose window, at 10m (32ft) in diameter the largest in England. It is supported outside by double flying buttresses and pinnacles that are 13m (42ft) high. The stone tracery, 46cm (18in) thick and weighing 52.8 tonnes (52 tons), contains 30,000 separate pieces of glass held together with generous leadwork and bronze stanchions.

The heraldic glass in the rose window symbolises the unity of the schools which were part of the Woodard Corporation in 1978. The shield of Lancing in the centre is surrounded by the motto of the Corporation. The petals of the inner rose (33–48) are filled with decorative ornament, leading to the arms of the dioceses (trefoils 17–32) in which the schools are situated. In the outer ring (1–16) are the arms of all the schools which contributed to the cost of the window, which was made by Mr A.E. Buss of Goddard and Gibbs Studios.

Key to the Rose Window

1	Hurstpierpoint	12	Saint Claire, Polwithen	23	Chester
2	Ardingly	13	Kings College, Taunton	24	Newcastle
3	Bloxham	14	Abbots Bromley	25	York
4	Saint Michael's, Petworth	15	Ellesmere	26	Ripon
5	Worksop	16	Denstone	27	Wakefield
6	Westwood House, Peterborough	17	Canterbury	28	Exeter
7	Saint Hilary's, Alderley Edge	18	Chichester	29	Bath and Wells
8	King's School, Tynemouth	19	Oxford	30	Truro
9	Queen Margaret's, York	20	Southwell	31	Llandaff
10	Queen Ethelburga's, Harrogate	21	Bury St Edmunds	32	Lichfield
11	Grenville College, Bideford	22	Peterborough	50	Lancing College

IN GRATEFUL REMEMBRANCE OF CANON ARTHUR RUPERT BROWNE-WILKINSON PROVOST 1944-1961

The Crypt

As you enter the crypt along its north aisle, there are various memorial windows and inscriptions. The three windows over the north door, designed by John Lawson, represent the three Sussex saints, Richard, Wilfrid and Cuthman, with details illustrating their lives. A sequence of Oberammergau stations of the cross begins here and follows round into the central crypt chapel. There are memorials and windows recording the school's nineteenth-century history and participation in the South African war.

Outside is a porch, realised by Alan Rome from the drawings of Carpenter's successor, Benjamin Ingelow, and built in 1993 to commemorate Basil Handford, former pupil, teacher, historian and benefactor of Lancing.

The north chapel, dedicated to All Saints, commemorates the Church in Korea, where several Old Boys have served, and the cathedral is dedicated to Saints Mary and Nicolas. The large stone with a cross is the foundation stone, laid by Bishop Gilbert of Chichester on 28 July 1868.

The central chapel is the Undercroft of Our Lady, recalling Lancing's association with the Shrine of Our Lady of Walsingham. The stained glass in the apse, by Clayton and Bell, is in memory of Herbert Carpenter, the architect. The stone altar, designed by Michael Drury, was built in 2004 and is in

memory of Bernard and Philippa Fielding and contains a relic of Saint John Bosco, a nineteenth-century Italian priest and educator. Here the Eucharist is celebrated daily in term time. The apse floor has recently been surfaced with Portland stone and Purbeck marble. The wrought-iron candlesticks are by Richard Bent.

On the south side is the All Souls Chapel, in African and Sicilian marbles with an alabaster reredos, designed by Ingelow to commemorate the Founder. There is a window showing Nathaniel Woodard offering up the chapel complete with its intended tower.

In the south-west bay, a side chapel dedicated to Saint Michael is in remembrance of Saint Michael's, Petworth, a former Woodard School. The riddel posts, Comper angels and oak kneelers were moved here from the high altar in the upper chapel to allow for westward celebration at the school Eucharist.

◁ Canon Browne-Wilkinson's memorial gates at the entrance to the crypt, designed by Dykes Bower.

▷ The central altar of the crypt apse, designed by Michael Drury; the windows are by Clayton and Bell.

The War Memorial Cloister

Visitors should approach the south cloister by way of the main drive and along the path which passes an RAFA garden of remembrance. The cloister was designed by Temple Moore and built between the wars by Dick Gale, last of the resident college masons. Note the window tracery and multipartite vault. The names of the fallen are engraved on slabs of pale Hoptonwood stone. In 2014, to mark the centenary of the First World War, a number of missing names were added, including a new plaque for members of the College Staff who were killed in action.

The east window, showing Saint Nicolas with three midshipmen, commemorates the use of the college by the Royal Navy during the Second World War. In the bay to the east of the cloister is the burial place of the Founder. Looking up from here at the great height of the chapel, where he himself set the topmost stone, you can appreciate the daring originality of Woodard's vision.

➤ Window in the Founder's Memorial Chapel showing Nathaniel Woodard offering up the completed chapel with the tower he originally wanted at the west end.

➤ The War Memorial Cloister, designed by Temple Moore and built by Dick Gale in the 1920s.

Prayer for The Friends of Lancing Chapel

Almighty God
through the hands of our Founder
and many benefactors
You have given us this house of prayer
as a symbol of your presence and your glory;
bless the work of the Friends of Lancing Chapel,
that guarding and enriching
what we have inherited,
we may do our part in making this building
so reflect the beauty of holiness
that many may be moved
to give their lives in your service
and become living stones in your eternal temple;
through Jesus Christ our Lord,
who is alive and reigns with you
and the Holy Spirit,
One God, for ever and ever.

+ Mark Green

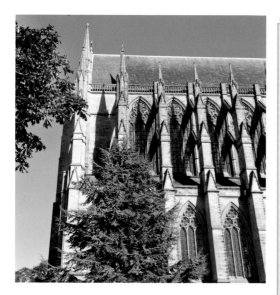

The south elevation, showing the flying buttresses and the unfinished west wall.

THE NEED FOR FUNDS

The building of Lancing Chapel is not yet complete. A porch is proposed for the west end. Meanwhile, routine maintenance and an essential programme of stone conservation are a constant expense. You may contribute by putting a donation in the safe on the pillar to the right of the sales table or by becoming a Friend of Lancing Chapel. There is an application form on the free welcome leaflet, or write to the Hon. Secretary of the Friends, Lancing College, Lancing, West Sussex BN15 0RW; friendsoflancingchapel@lancing.org.uk

Acknowledgements

Written (1982) and revised (1992, 2006 and 2014) by Jeremy Tomlinson
© The Friends of Lancing Chapel
Photographs by Heather Hook © The Friends of Lancing Chapel, except for IFC and p.1 (both), supplied by Lancing College.
Publication in this form © Pitkin Publishing 2014.
ISBN 978-1-84165-594-9   1/14
Pitkin Publishing, The History Press, The Mill, Brimscombe Port, Stroud, Gloucestershire, GL5 2QG.

PITKIN

ISBN: 978-1-84165-594-9

9 781841 655949